27 Things You Need to Be Aware of Before You Start Trading the Forex

By Steve Rising

ISBN 978-1-105-864834

All Rights Reserved ©2012 Steve Rising Publications. First Printing: 2012. The editorial arrangement, analysis, and professional commentary are subject to this copyright notice. No portion of this book may be copied, retransmitted, reposted, duplicated, or otherwise used without the express written approval of the author.

Any unauthorized copying, reproduction, translation, or distribution of any part of this material without permission by the author is prohibited and against the law.

Reliance upon information contained in this material is solely at the reader's own risk.

Table of Contents

Introduction

Today's Global Marketplace

The Impact of Electronic Trading

Is Forex Trading for Me?

How to Succeed in Forex Trading

Common Sense Forex Trading

How to Find Time to Trade the Forex

Welcome to the World's Most Lucrative Market

Becoming a Profitable Forex Trader

Process First, Performance Second

In Poker They Call It Tilt

The World's Greatest Trading Indicator

The Reality of Using Technical Indicators to Trade the Forex

Forex Trading: Price Action vs. Technical Indicator

Trend Following vs. Scalping

The Dynamics of Daily Forex Price Activity

Trend or Range?

The Fibonacci Trading Myth

The Power of Simplicity

In Search of Sasquatch, the Loch Ness Monster, Forex Robots and Other Great Myths

Key Elements Today's Forex Trader Needs To Be Versed In

Forex Trader vs. Forex Investor

Low Risk Forex Trading

Forex Trading Using Technical Analysis

Trade the Forex with the Correct Time Frame

Three Things That Will Make You a Solid Forex Trader

Learn to Trade the Forex: The 3 Steps to a Profitable Trade

The Range and Reversal Trade

Warning: Not Everyone Is Capable of Becoming a Solid Forex Trader

Introduction

Eighty percent of those who pursue trading will fail in their first year. The reason for this is that most folks have a huge misconception as to what the daily function of a stand-alone trader is. Let me break it down for you. Your job as a solo trader is to watch, analyze, wait, continue to watch, continue to wait, and finally execute on a specific pattern with a high probability of success on a consistent basis.

Your job is to look for that recurring high probability pattern and <u>decide whether to trade your capital or wait</u> on the sidelines. That is your job. You are not a micro-economist. You are not an analyst. It is that simple.

Unfortunately the 80% believe that trading is simply a process of logging into their trading platform and then reviewing some information, typically a combination of both fundamental and technical. Based on that quick review they then make what they believe is an educated guess on the direction price is going to move and then place a trade. As soon as the trade is placed, the novice trader then hopes he is lucky enough to make a profit.

By the way, the gambler goes through almost the exact same steps when deciding what number to bet on when playing roulette. Flipping a coin would probably yield better results.

The key point to remember is that those high probability trading conditions may not be occurring every time you decide you feel like trading.

Remember: Your job as a solo trader is to watch, analyze, wait, continue to watch, continue to wait, and finally execute on a specific pattern with a high probability of success on a consistent basis.

This compendium was written to keep you out of the 80%. Learning to trade is just like learning any other discipline. It requires a training phase where you learn to understand the daily dynamics of the particular market you are interested in trading which in this case is the forex.

Trading is not a complex process. Just like learning any other discipline it requires the repetitive process of practice. Ultimately you are learning to identify a core set of high probability conditions that occur regularly in order to trade successfully.

The "keep it simple" approach is a solid foundation to work from. Another common reason for inconsistent performance is simply gathering too much information. The premise here is to learn to eliminate the unnecessary information and focus on only the necessary information.

This compendium was written in a format that allows the reader to either read from beginning to end or to select a topic and then read the information under that topic as a stand-alone source.

The information pertaining to each topic was purposely written in a concise straight-forward format. The reader is encouraged to read the same information a few times.

As in all new disciplines your mental approach is critical, trading being no different. A lot of the topics pertain to trader psychology and learning to control your emotions. Ninety percent of becoming a solid trader is training yourself to stick to your rules. As humans the way we become disciplined is by habit. The way we develop a new habit is through repetition.

The reality is, learning what to trade is the simple part. Training yourself to wait for the correct conditions to develop is the hard part. Just as the athlete trains constantly so that when game time comes he can keep his emotions in check, so should the solid trader.

Remember successful traders will do what unsuccessful traders refuse to do. Successful traders understand that discipline is the bedrock of their success.

Today's Global Marketplace

The global marketplace is changing rapidly. The way we trade is changing as well.

- Daily volatility on the Dow is increasing.

- Gold maintains historical highs.

- The housing mortgage disaster.

- The fed continues to cut rates.

- The value of the dollar continues to diminish.

Investors and traders are experiencing greater volatility more frequently across all markets.

In the past volatility was perceived as a negative. However, market volatility can be a good thing if you have the correct training and are in the right market.

To the experienced trader volatility equates to more opportunities allowing one to achieve one's profit objective in a shorter period of time.

It is apparent that, with easy access to information and online access to the markets, more people are getting into the markets and holding positions for shorter periods of time which is stimulating greater volatility and greater liquidity.

It would be great if one could take advantage of these conditions with minimal time commitment and minimal capital. Well, you can in the forex market. Individuals are able to capitalize on fractional moves in this market place with as little as $250 of capital. Additionally, the forex market is the largest and the fastest growing market in the world.

Most people are typically unable to take advantage of these market opportunities because they do not have the necessary resources - time and money.

Now with easy online access to the world's most lucrative market, this is changing. With the correct training, one can spend just a few hours a day a few days a week with minimal capital looking for short-term profitable opportunities in the currency markets.

The Impact of Electronic Trading

Did you ever think that these things would be replaced to the point of becoming obsolete?

Mail replaced with email.

Home phone replaced with cell phone.

Printed media replaced with e-media.

Exchange-traded or open outcry markets replaced with electronic trading.

Did you know that electronic trading has changed the way individuals make money in all markets? The trading techniques profitable today where not even around 5 years ago. Because of electronic trading, markets have greater volatility, which means price moves faster and changes direction more frequently. There are fewer and fewer moves that are based on trend-related activities.

Conventional wisdom 10 years ago was that the trend is your friend. Today with the impact of technology and a global economy, this is an outdated trading technique. Dramatic market swings are now an everyday occurrence in all markets.

Technical indicators that were developed to assist the trader in trending conditions are no longer effective in the majority of today's day to day price action.

The trader who wants to be successful moving forward needs to look at these changes from the perspective of, how do these changes undermine my current way of thinking? Not from the perspective, how do these changes help my current way of thinking?

The typical mindset is that changes in market dynamics due to electronic trading and the new global economy can be bolted to traditional old economy pre-electronic trading processes. In fact, those old processes need to be discarded.

Short-term trading or scalping was considered too risky 5 years ago. Now staying in the market for extended periods of time is the riskier methodology, due to the **instantaneous** impact of changes in price direction brought on by electronic trading.

If your perception is that dramatic swings in the market are a bad thing, it is because you are stuck in the past. Regardless of the market, electronic trading is here to stay and will only continue to grow. Stop looking for trend driven activity and focus on quick momentum based moves.

There has never been a better time to learn to trade a solid scalping technique. Scalp trading requires less time in the market and allows one to trade with minimal risk because of this. Another concern is the amount of profit one can make. With scalp trading you can realize the same profit in a shorter period of time simply by trading multiple lots.

Is Forex Trading for Me?

Before you make any commitment to begin trading, I believe you must honestly ask yourself, "Is forex trading for me?"

Many programs will tell you anyone can make money trading the currency markets. But the reality is, for most, failure is inevitable.

Why do so many people fail at trading? The short answer is - no training.

90% of trading is psychological; the other 10% is technical knowledge. So your success is based on how you approach becoming a trader.

Here are the three primary reasons why those who pursue trading fail:

- Lack of commitment.

- Lack of knowledge.

- Their egos get in the way.

Traders who don't address these issues will not survive. Statistics show this to be true.

Commitment:

Commitment is critical. Most become frustrated because they do not realize instant success. In fact this holds true in any new pursuit. The average person quits early in the game solely because of lack of commitment and unrealistic expectation of immediate success.

Knowledge:

Lack of knowledge, which is a major cause of failure, is a result of an individual's attitude. How anyone thinks they can trade the currency market without professional training amazes me. Yet it happens all the time. People who accept that golf lessons are necessary before they head out onto the course will start trading with little or no knowledge. Because you are reading this I assume you do not share that view. This is a major step in the right direction. Most traders fail to appreciate the level of skill needed to trade successfully. They have no foundation in how to understand price activity. They do not have a set of rules or guidelines. It is amazing how many individuals develop a trading strategy by gleaning free information off the internet. In actuality, all these individuals are doing is gambling.

Another common mistake is gathering too much information. It is statistically proven that if you narrow your focus, you have a higher probability of success. It is critical at this juncture not to confuse information with knowledge.

Ego:

Ego is one of the greatest enemies to a trader's success. Your ego needs to win all the time and wants to win now. It can't stand being wrong. And so it rationalizes events and denies reality. You must be able to perceive the market as it is, not how you want to believe it is. It is difficult to clearly see price action if your ego is in the way. Ego makes us take small profits but large losses. It argues that even a small profit is a win. But a loss hurts and instead of accepting a small loss we try and get it back. Ego is why we hold onto bad trades that end up being even bigger losing trades.

Without action, knowledge is useless. Massive action is the key to real success. Many begin with great enthusiasm but become easily disillusioned. Perseverance is required to get beyond this stage and to start reaping the rewards.

As Aristotle said, "We are what we repeatedly do. Excellence, therefore, is not an act but a habit".

How to Succeed in Forex Trading

Forex trading is fast becoming a career alternative for many individuals, as it should. It offers flexible hours, work from home option, and high income potential.

What is the reality of trading?

Trading is like any other business. Did you know that about 80% of all new businesses fail within the first year? The failure is typically based on just a few reasons - under capitalization, lack of a sound business plan or inexperienced management. Any one of these can cause a business to fail. However individuals still pursue business ownership.

The same holds true for trading. A trader may fail because of the same reasons - under capitalization, no clear trading plan, poor management skills, and lack of discipline.

What is the right way to succeed?

Find the correct trading methodology. In other words, work off of a successful business plan. The reason new business owners are willing to pay additional dollars for a franchise is because a franchise offers a tried and true business plan.

The novice business owner with little or no experience who tries by trial and error will, statistical speaking, fail. So holds true for the novice trader who tries to develop a trading methodology with zero knowledge and experience. Did you know that most people believe they will become successful traders by using free information obtained off the internet? Trading is simply a discipline. Learning a discipline requires a specific process. Having access to a coach or mentor is critical.

With easy access to the necessary technology, forex trading offers a rewarding, lucrative income alternative for any individual. In comparison to brick and mortar business ownership, the startup costs are minimal.

Common Sense Forex Trading

Percentage of accuracy is an obsession of novice traders. But it is not a very important criterion for judging a trading indicator. Some highly effective models are wrong more often than right, while some marginal models are right more often than they are wrong. The best advice is to "keep it simple". Nothing is a better indicator than a price chart. When looking for a trading program, you need to first establish realistic objectives that are right for you. Remember a trading system designed for a well-capitalized long-term investor wanting to ride long-term trends will not work for an undercapitalized speculator looking for quick profits with minimal risk.

The big investor can handle large draw downs (negative positions) that very frequently and typically occur when trend trading. The trader with limited capital needs to find profit in the smaller price movements that occur on short-term time frames. This individual needs a sensitive, accurate program that can offer consistent profitability. Smaller gains, but more frequent ones.

Both traders need to manage their capital accordingly. The big trader will trade less frequently. The smaller trader will trade more frequently but must cut losses immediately. Trend trading is easy. Anyone with a good long-term chart and a decent book can trade a trend. Short term trading requires the individual to develop the ability to learn how to understand and interpret price activity.

If you want to be successful you must study and learn. You cannot simply buy someone else's technology and blindly rely on it.

Short-term traders need to first adopt a specific set of rules that are learned and then internalized. This builds confidence, which then develops quality experiences. Then the ability to utilize technology comes into play.

A short-term trader needs to first develop the ability to trade a stand-alone pricing chart consistently before considering moving forward and adding on additional analytical tools. Unfortunately most individuals do not take this path. Most pursue a program that is typically trend based and try to make it work with less capital on a smaller time frame only to end up wasting valuable time and money.

All short-term traders need to develop the ability to trade based solely on price action, before getting involved with more sophisticated processes.

How to Find Time to Trade the Forex

Have an interest in trading the forex market? However you may feel you don't have the necessary time.

Here are the three biggest myths about the amount of time it takes to learn and then trade the forex:

1. You have to spend countless hours in front of your computer.

Nothing could be farther from the truth. In fact, a primary reason traders fail is because they spend too much time watching the market. Being glued to your computer is a bad thing. You read into things and make poor decisions.

One cardinal rule to follow is to "plan your trade, trade your plan." All it takes is blocking out 30-45 minutes each day. This could be in the morning, afternoon or night. At a convenient time, use a planning worksheet to create a trading plan. Once this is done, you can set an alarm on your trading platform that will email you or send you a text message alerting you to a potential trading opportunity.

2. I presently work so I cannot pursue the training process.

First, select the correct training environment. Look for programs that offer unlimited access. This means you can pursue the training at your own pace. When developing any new skill it is best to commit just a couple of hours per day 2-3 days per week. The individuals who overdo it and pursue an intensive crash course style of training always run into problems.

Statistically, the individuals who are currently working while pursuing a training process to learn how to trade do better because they approach the training process in a conservative fashion.

Secondly, look for training that is online. Classroom training with a fixed schedule is archaic. Online training allows you to have 7 day a week 24 hour a day to access via an online learning center. Unlimited access means a flexible training process tailored to your schedule.

3. Because of my job I need to trade on a large time frame.

Keep in mind that the forex market is open 5 days a week 24 hours a day. It has incredible volatility. Most individual traders get slaughtered trying to stay in this market for an extended period of time trading on larger time frames (15 minutes or greater).

Here is the reality: Once you are in the market, as the hours pass the concern for your trade creates so much anxiety that you continually need to check on it throughout that time. The result: lost sleep, distracted at work. This particular myth is why so many fail.

Select a trading methodology that allows you to be in and out of the market in most cases in under an hour. Imagine this scenario. You create your plan at your own convenience. Hours later you receive a text message alerting you to a potential money making opportunity. You go online, set your trading order, 40-60 minutes later the trade is done. Profit achieved!

No lost sleep. No distractions while you are working. The reality is that trading on a small time frame works best for a working individual. It is the person with time on their hands that can trade on larger time frames. Here is another reality. Most people find they do not want to be in the market for extended periods of time because of the anxiety involved.

Sometimes a paradigm shift or a shift in our preconceived ideas is all it takes to see new opportunities in front of us. We all have one thing in common. We all have 24 hours a day. All it takes is learning new ways to manage that time to create additional opportunities for ourselves.

Welcome to the World's Most Lucrative Market

Did you know that the forex is the largest market on the planet? Daily volume is currently reaching US$4 trillion compared to the New York Stock Exchange which only has an average daily volume of US$1.9 billion. In fact, the combination of all of the major exchanges on the planet still does not come close to the daily volume of the forex.

The forex is also the fastest growing market on the planet, with the majority of growth being comprised of individual traders. The reason the forex is growing so rapidly and attracting individual traders is because it is the perfect market to trade on an intra-day basis.

Did you know that the forex market is the world's most volatile market? In the past, conventional wisdom was that volatility meant greater risk so most folks steered away from volatile markets. Now with instant online access, the more volatile the conditions the more opportunities there are to trade.

One of the key characteristics of the forex that is different from other markets is that the directional bias of an individual currency pair changes frequently, meaning the trader can be planning for a long trade in the morning, then planning a short trade on the very same pair in the afternoon.

Once the trader begins to understand this unique characteristic of forex price action, he is on the way to becoming a solid, consistent trader. One of the reasons many folks struggle to become a consistent trader is they attempt to use trading techniques that work in the stock or futures market but do not work in the forex because of this consistent shift in the direction of the price.

In other words, each individual currency pair is typically in a range or sideways the majority of the time. Because of this consistent range-bound price action, one needs to be versed in a solid scalping technique to consistently make profitable trades. The benefit is there are plenty of opportunities to trade in a 24 hour period and the trader does not have to stay in a trade for extended periods of time. What that means is less risk and more consistent profit taking.

Combining huge amounts of volume with lots of volatility equals frequent, profitable trading opportunities with minimal risk for the forex trader using a scalping technique.

It is a simple process of trading multiple lots (on average 3 to 5 lots) and establishing a net 10 pip profit target to make $300 to $500 on a trade in less than 30 minutes.

Becoming a Profitable Forex Trader

How many people do you know of who have lost money trading the forex market or the stock market? Chances are you've probably heard or know of someone who has dabbled in the markets as a day-trader without long term success or even some devastating losses in a relatively short period.

Not many would argue against saying that the most common reason why trading is so difficult for so many people is that it's so hard to emotionally detach yourself from the price action when you're sitting in front of your computer. The movement of the charts is fun to watch, even mesmerizing at times. It's hard not to jump in when you see the price ticks go up and up, at once beguiling and challenging you to get in on the action.

But it takes more than just the ability to click on a mouse to make consistent profits in the trading game. You know that, but just knowing that and knowing how to make it happen day in and day out are two very different things. What is required for the latter to become reality? It requires using a solid, proven trading process.

Most folks typically start out using indicator-based trading processes and 80-90% of those who do, fail in their first year. That does not mean that they never have a profitable trade. What it means is that they continually give back profits and ultimately the losing trades outpace the winning trades. At the end of the first year, their trading results are in the negative.

The trader that follows a specific set of rules or a trading methodology typically performs better. The reason is that they follow the same black and white steps each and every time they plan for trading setups. Over time, they begin to develop a skill because they understand what they are doing right and, more importantly, what they are doing wrong. This way, they do not repeat the same mistakes over and over.

The trader who uses a rule-based trading methodology knows exactly why they are considering a particular trading setup. Most indicator-based traders hope all the stars are aligned and are trading on "blind faith". The primary reason for this is that indicators are lagging. In other words, they tell us what has already happened. Using a rule-based trading methodology, the trader is interpreting price action. Price action is the only predictive indicator that works consistently.

A proven formula for success is a proper understanding and application of a solid trading methodology, consistent practice, and correct application of that methodology.

A proven forex trading methodology is Thinslice Trading ® available at:

www.theforextradinginstitute.com

Process First, Performance Second

The reality is that we can achieve practically any goal we establish if we are realistic about the process of what it takes to achieve it.

Becoming a successful forex trader is a goal that most anyone can accomplish. However, I believe, once again, you must be realistic to achieve this goal. I stress this point of being realistic; the single biggest reason individuals do not become successful as traders is because of an unrealistic expectation.

Typically, individuals who become involved in trading pursue and evaluate products based solely on performance or the potential profit and not the process of what it takes to achieve that performance. It is unfortunate when you interact with individuals who believe success is going to come in 30 days or less.

I recommend to those who want to become successful traders to put primary emphasis on the importance of the process because we know success will naturally follow. But once again, the process has to be realistic.

Let me give you this analogy. A few years ago, I made the decision that I wanted to complete a marathon, specifically the New York City Marathon. Now, I was never a runner. I have always been active and athletic, but long distance running was a new endeavor.

First thing I did towards completing a marathon was to establish a time frame of one year to train. A common reason people fail to achieve their goal, especially traders, is impatience and not allocating a realistic period of time to achieve the goal.

The training process was a simple formula: small realistic objectives, repeating over and over until my body and brain were conditioned to obtain those objectives as part of my regular routine. Once I was conditioned to the point of habit, I increased the size of my objective.

Continuous weekly repetition was the foundation to assuring I would achieve the goal. I had to condition myself mentally first, allow time to pass and continue to run regularly, and then I gradually became physically conditioned.

My point is that, each time I increased my distance the true obstacle did not become physical but mental. My body was used to running 5 miles every other day. When I decided to increase to 7 miles, my brain would transmit signals for me to stop. Now, it was only 2 additional miles. If I had been running regular 5 mile increments for 90 days, adding 2 more miles was not unrealistic. But once again, I had to change my mental outlook; the physical aspects developed naturally.

The process was the key to my success. It was my ability to continue to improve my performance and set realistic objectives over a realistic period of time that was critical. In fact, I knew naturally when I was ready to increase the distance. It was easy. I became used to the current distance I was at and it had become second nature. It was this conditioning in the process that made it clear it was time to raise the bar. One year later, I completed the marathon. Did I come in 1st place, no. Did I come in last place, no. I was right in the median, at the realistic expectation I had set. The process was all I focused on. The goal (performance) was achieved as a result of the process.

During the course of my training, I adjusted my diet, took supplements, and learned about how I should adjust my stride. I had a clear foundation of the why's and how's of what I needed to do to become successful, and then I set a sensible time to achieve my goal and I never once tried to hurry the process. I also never suffered any injury. Some weeks I needed to take off. Once again, I was following the correct process over time and the performance naturally followed.

Becoming a successful forex trader is no different. You need a foundation and understanding of price movement. Then you just need to give yourself enough time to condition yourself to see the good setups versus the bad setups. Your performance will continue to improve and so too will your profits.

That's why individuals who want to become successful traders should focus on training first. Commonly most believe they can find a shortcut that will allow them to make large profits, when in fact it is the training process that ensures your success.

That process is train, train, train, practice, practice, practice. This takes a combination of two things. With the discipline of training and practicing on a regular basis, and the passage of time, your success will naturally follow.

Most of the questions that I am typically asked are all performance based, such as, "How many trades a day? How much money can I make in a week?" and so on.

With the correct training, with the most important part being the mental conditioning, all of these issues become moot because you learn market conditions are ever changing. Some weeks yield more profit than others. But, it does not matter because if you focus on the process, continually improving your trading acumen, your success will naturally improve as well.

Focus on the process first, and then performance simply becomes a result of a sound process.

In Poker They Call It Tilt

In poker they call it "tilt" when poker players let their emotions cloud their poker judgment. Traders suffer from tilt as well. In fact, statistics show that 90% of trading is learning to control your emotions.

Alex Honnold, the record-breaking free solo climber, said "There is no adrenaline rush...if I get a rush, it means that something has gone horribly wrong...the whole thing should be pretty slow and controlled."

The exact same thing can be said about trading. If you are trading correctly, you should not feel your adrenaline flowing as the market moves up or down. You should be calmly watching as the price moves towards your target price, as you take your profit, and as you exit the market. Why? Because the whole process was expected, planned and executed as planned.

There are a number of ways one can learn to control emotions. The one that makes the most sense is to get proper training so that you gain the correct knowledge and experience. In other words, you know what you're doing. Your trades are executed based on a solid understanding of price action in a particular market.

The emotion-free trader works from a base of trading rules, just as the emotion-free gamer does. By working from this core set of rules, the trader or the gamer can identify a solid trade or play. As experience accumulates, both the trader and the gamer understand winning scenarios versus losing scenarios.

The trader's number one rule should be to "always look for reasons not to place a trade."

As logical as it sounds, the reality is that most folks do not follow this common sense approach. In fact, 9 out of 10 people attempt to become successful traders by following the gambler's approach. A simple definition of the gambler's approach is attempting to find some process or tool that will allow the trader to make the quickest profit with the least amount of effort. It really does defy common sense that someone would be able to buy something for a few hundred bucks that would allow them to make huge profits with little to no effort.

But go on the internet right now and you will find hundreds if not thousands of trading products selling this concept. The unfortunate part of this real-world situation is that 90% of those folks who call themselves traders purchase these products. Even worse, they purchase a number of these products before reality sinks in.

The rational for purchasing these types of programs is, "well, it's just a few hundred dollars. I will give it a try and hope I am lucky". Those two words are the foundation of the gambling trader's mantra, "hope" and "luck."

The skilled trader relies on knowledge and experience which we all know takes some time to obtain. Just as the solid poker player seeks out training, mentoring and coaching to avoid making common gambler mistakes, the solid forex trader needs to pursue the same path.

A simple rule of thumb to follow to become a solid forex trader is to not do what the losing 90% are doing. Do what the winning 10% are doing. If it sounds too good to be true, it is!

There are no such things as secrets to becoming a solid forex trader. The solid forex trader pursues the same path you would take to become proficient at any discipline. Become properly trained.

The World's Greatest Trading Indicator

It seems that we now only put value on complexity or what we often label as "advanced". The buzzword today in trading is "indicators, indicators, indicators". Which one is the best?

The mentality seems to be that if I can use a remote control to turn on my TV then I should be able to find similar technology as a trading solution, because a computer can solve anything if it is programmed correctly, right? So far, not to date.

Remember if there was a way to "figure out the market", there would be no market. Think about it.

In other words, instead of trying to solve it, you should approach trading with the correct mindset. How can I get involved, survive, and then ultimately take a profit?

Let me table this concept. Unfortunately it is not my own. However, I am duty bound to pass it on:

> Any intelligent fool can make things more complex and harder to solve. It is the genius who is willing to go in the opposite direction. Remember, genius is the ability to make the complex simple.

This is not to take away from gentlemen like George Lane who developed the stochastic oscillator. The stochastic measures a closing price in relation to the price range over a period of time. Don't get me wrong. The stochastic process has a place in trading. But where is that place? After all, it is measuring the relationship between price and time. So what else shows us the relationship between price and time? The answer is a price chart.

The novice will use the stochastic to try to figure out the market. The experienced trader will use it as a tool in his decision making process. But how much value should he place on it? Does he use it as the leading criterion in his trading decisions? Answer, no.

What is the world's greatest indicator? The leader is simply price. All other indicators should follow in importance. The application is, as always, price and time. Is this indicator being applied to a suitable timeframe and pricing range? You will not know that answer until you learn to understand how to evaluate the relationship between price and time by using only price as the indicator, first and foremost.

Trading is just like any other discipline. The formula for success is four simple steps:

1. Train.

2. Practice (this is where you gain experience).

3. Implement.

4. Repeat.

The Reality of Using Technical Indicators to Trade the Forex

The primary difference between intra-day price action in the forex market compared to that in the equities market or the futures market is that the directional bias of each currency pair changes frequently. Once a trader understands this condition, he begins to realize that many of the techniques used to trade in other markets do not perform consistently when trading a currency pair in the forex market.

Statistically, in the beginning of traders' careers (the first 24 months or so), the standard direction the majority takes is to attempt to trade technical indicators. The reality is that the majority cannot trade with indicators and realize a consistent profit. Once again, I emphasize that it is "consistent profit". I am repeating this because it is a common practice in the first year of a trader's career to have selective memory and focus on the day, the week, or the isolated month that a profit was realized.

I am aware that "marketing hype" may lead one to believe otherwise. The reality is that most people do not really get serious until they have been burned a few times from the marketing hype, or they simply quit.

The first "aha" moment for the trader is somewhere in the second year. The "aha" is that he realizes the potential to generate an income trading is there, but the ability to do so by solely relying on indicators or a stand-alone technology is not the answer.

Now don't get me wrong, indicators do have a place in trading, but it is a very specific place. First, indicators perform best when the entity that is being traded is in a trending condition. Because of the constant shift in the directional bias in each currency pair, that "trending condition" exists less than 20% of the time in the forex.

What this means to the trader is that when using indicators to identify profitable setups, those setups are going to occur infrequently. In fact, computer models show that when using a simple moving average or a combination of SMA's, a profitable setup will occur once every 42 days.

So the solution has been to attempt to develop an indicator that will find more frequent setups. The outcome is that the more frequently an indicator trades the percentage of accuracy declines. The exponential moving average is an excellent example of this concept. Frequency of setups increases to a setup every 6 days, but only 4 out of every 10 trades is profitable. What this means is that false signals increase. False signals for the trader are a nightmare because the only thing that identifies a false signal is a trading loss. He realizes it is false only after the trade is made.

The second "aha" moment for the trader is when he realizes he needs to learn how to trade technical price patterns, not technical indicators. There is a huge difference. The harsh reality is, statistically the majority quit before they realize that second "aha" moment.

There are literally hundreds and hundreds of price patterns and volumes of books on technical patterns. The intra-day forex trader can weed out 95% of those patterns. The reason: 95% of the patterns are only applicable in a trending condition, meaning most of the patterns occur infrequently.

This is where getting professional training and learning a specific methodology comes in. A methodology is a rule-based trading application that teaches the forex trader how to identify the most frequently occurring technical price pattern and, more importantly, the pattern with the highest probability to achieve the intended profit objective.

A rule-based trading application is an algorithmic process. Now I know that sounds complex. It is not. The definition of an algorithm is a step by step procedure one follows to achieve an intended outcome.

This is the third "aha" moment for the trader. Remember, this trader now represents the survivor, the one who goes on to become a consistent trader. He realizes that, to be consistent, he needs to follow a very black and white, step-by-step trading process.

Forex Trading: Price Action vs. Technical Indicator

Most traders are under the misconception that using technical indicators makes trading easier, the belief being that indicators represent some type of technological advancement that allows anyone to solve the mystery of which direction the market is going to move with zero market experience.

Building on that misconception, the next step is to believe the more indicators one uses the greater accuracy one can trade at. Because of these misconceptions, most folks begin and end their trading career using some mix of indicators.

Remember, 80% fail at trading and statistics show most of these failed traders are using indicators.

In order to become a successful trader, it is imperative that one not do what the 80% are doing.

The majority of the most frequently used indicators are simply some form of a collection of pricing data that creates a numerical point. One can then plot that point across a chart so that one can see some form of a price average, or that point is automatically plotted on a chart in a pleasing color that the trader selects.

The problem with this is that all indicators are lagging because the numbers have to be generated first such that the formula driving the indicator can crunch those numbers and come up with a result to plot. By the time that number is derived the market has already moved on. In short, indicators tell us what has already happened. Indicators are not predicative and only tell us what the overall tendency of price movement has been.

What this means is that indicators perform best on large time frames and are better used for investing and/or buy-and-hold scenarios. When indicators are used on smaller time frames, for instance on an intra-day basis, the changes in the direction in price happen too quickly for the indicator to alert the trader.

When indicators are adjusted to supposedly work on smaller time frames, accuracy diminishes and frequent false signals occur. The trader cannot determine a false signal until after it has happened and then it is too late. By that point he has lost money.

Indicators do not perform well in highly volatile conditions or in fast moving markets. The forex market is the most volatile market on the planet. Directional bias changes frequently and rapidly. These are the two toughest conditions for indicators to consistently perform, hence the high failure rate of forex traders who rely on indicators.

The single best attribute of indicator trading is that it is an easy sell. Marketing the power of indicators by looking at after-the-fact pricing data (back-testing) lures one to believe that all they have to do is purchase the proprietary indicator package or system, turn it on, and the dollars are just going to start rolling in. You have seen the "hypothetical results". Using technology eliminates human emotions. Technology is not as error prone as human interface. The benefits that are marketed are endless and all the benefits point to "easy money".

If indicators, indicator based systems, and software based trading programs (these programs rely on the same processes that drive indicators) are so great, why are 80%-90% not able to grow their trading accounts in a positive direction using these trading tools? Why do the statistics show that the majority of traders who attempt to use these technology based trading processes always end up giving back any profits they may have gleaned on a few isolated profitable trades, and then finally quit?

The answer is simple. Eight out of 10 individuals fail to realize that to become a solid trader one has to follow the same path that any individual would follow to insure their success in any professional endeavor. They need to be trained. They need to get experience. The training takes time because they have to be exposed to various market conditions and experiences and then must learn from those experiences.

Eight out of 10 are looking for something that does not exist. If becoming a solid trader simply required you to spend some money on a class that you only had to attend one time for a day or two or even three and then you were off making money, everyone would do it.

The reality is simple: 80% will spend anywhere from $2,000 to $10,000 on average over a year or two on gimmicks and schemes that pitch instant money making trading opportunities, then quit with the misconception that the market is "rigged".

These folks were living in total denial, never realizing that they simply took a gambler's approach. Remember, gamblers rely on hope and luck. These folks purchased all of this trading garbage hoping that one of the products purchased would create the luck they needed to make that "fast money".

Solid traders understand that learning to trade is a skill, a skill that takes a little time to develop. The first step is learning to trade solely off of price action. Price action is the only predictive tool a trader has. By learning to interpret price action, the trader learns what conditions need to develop to place a trade. More importantly, he learns what not to trade. The solid trader would prefer to evaluate the conditions and determine a no-trading condition. The gambler always wants to be trading.

The comparisons are easy to see. There is the guy who goes into a casino with a fist full of dollars with no clear direction relying solely on hope and luck to make money versus the professional gamer who waits for high probability conditions to develop before putting money on the line.

The same reasons most fail in Las Vegas are the same reasons most folks are failed traders. They have zero discipline or commitment to take the time to properly learn what it takes to be successful at either endeavor.

The solid trader understands that price action works differently in different markets. In order to effectively trade the forex, one needs to be properly trained on how to interpret forex price action. This is why stock traders get hammered when they first attempt to trade the forex.

Eventually one realizes that price action is the only truly reliable indicator that a trader can work from. Anything else just creates additional layers of "noise" and complexities that do not generate more income.

The 20% that are successful rely on price action first, and as their individual trading styles develop, and based on what markets they trade, indicators may be used as a secondary tool. Indicators are never a primary tool.

To be in the 20%, you need to realize that whichever tool you use, price action or an indicator, they both require time and experience to use effectively. Learning to trade price action is easier than learning to use technical indicators. Unfortunately, interpreting price action by many is perceived as less glamorous than having your trading platform loaded up with a multitude of colorful indicators and histograms.

The bottom line is, if you are serious about making money you will focus on what the 20% do, not what the 80% do. This means that if the tool or method is available for free, mainstream, or defies common sense, it is highly probable that it does not work and that the losing 80% are using it regularly.

Trend Following vs. Scalping

Let's take a quick history lesson on trading.

Trend following has been around for decades. Because of this, there is decades of information about trend following. That is why trend following is so popular. There is a direct relationship to the increase in individuals getting involved in the markets to the increase in the flow of market information to individuals. Hence, most individuals that started trading in markets typically became trend followers. Because of this circular growth in trend following, trend following became a self-fulfilling prophecy.

But decades ago, markets had to be viewed from a much different perspective than they are now.

Fast forward to today. Internet access changes the face of trading. Online trading begins to emerge. Without online access, the only traders that could take advantage of smaller intra-day moves in the market place were floor traders. Now with online access, anyone can take advantage of these intra-day moves, otherwise known as scalping.

Online trading was not very popular until high speed internet access became widely accessible. It was in the mid 2000's, or about 5 years ago, when high speed internet began to become readily available.

Online trading is now the fastest growing segment of all markets. Because online trading is relatively new, so too is scalp trading. This means that there are mountains of information about trend trading, but relatively little information available about scalping.

This also means that "old school" traders put more stock in trend following techniques than scalping techniques. In other words, they are stuck in the past. One of the key advantages of scalping over trend following is that there is less risk in scalping because you can trade using very small stops.

Scalping suits most people better than trend following because:

- Scalping has less risk.

- You can trade with smaller amounts of money.

- You can achieve a profit in a shorter period of time.

- Scalpers sleep better because they are not in a trade overnight.

Because scalping is still relatively new, most individuals attempt to trade a trend following technique and scale it down to a smaller time frame to trade on an intra-day basis. That process does not yield consistent profits over time. But this is the direction most people take because there is more information available on trend following than scalping.

A common mistake the self-taught or trial and error trader makes is to co-mingle strategies and techniques ultimately becoming what I have labeled the 50/50 trader. Sometimes things work and sometimes they do not, which means trading performance was based on more luck than skill. As a scalper, you do not use any trend following techniques.

To properly scalp trade, you have to be careful what type of information you are viewing, since 90% of the available information is founded on trend following. Once again, that is where most start and why they are not successful attempting to scalp trade.

Scalpers need lots of volatility. Scalpers want the directional bias of the market to be changing constantly.

Trend followers steer away from volatility. Trend followers need the directional bias of the market they are trading to be consistent.

Trend followers cannot trade in range-bound conditions. Trend followers typically have more losing trades than winning trades. They need the one winning trade to overcome several losing trades.

Scalpers love range bound conditions and can trade in either trending or range-bound condition. Scalpers have more winning trades than losing trades. That keeps the trader in a positive frame of mind.

The forex is the perfect market for scalp trading. The forex is the most volatile market on the planet. This equates to more trading opportunities for the scalper. The forex is range-bound 80% of the time and trending 20% of the time.

To use a trend following technique trading the forex, you have to use extremely large stops because of the consistent range bound condition that occurs. Because of the large stops (greater risk), trend following requires trading accounts in excess of $25,000 in order to be aligned with sound equity management principles.

If a currency pair moves 75-100 pips a day, how easy would it be to find one 15 pip move? This would equal a net 10 pip profit on average. How would you like to make $500 in less than 30 minutes, instead of 6-8 hours? Scalpers do that. Trend followers typically hold onto trades for days or weeks or months.

There is also a higher probability that you will be able to find a net 10 pip move daily than a 100 pip move. This means less stress and anxiety. Technology now makes scalping possible. We are now at a point where telephone access via a landline for the individual is at a decline. Wireless phone technology has overtaken old telephone technology. Trend following is a dated style of trading. Scalping is on the leading edge of technology.

Trade 5 lots on one net 10 pip trade and that equals $500 in less than 60 minutes, instead of days or weeks or months in a trade with drawdowns. There is simply no need to trend follow in the forex market. You can make the same money in less time.

So you may ask, then why are not more people scalp traders?

Mindset!

The Dynamics of Daily Forex Price Activity

One key distinction between the ways in which price moves in the forex market versus other markets is that the directional bias is constantly changing. What this means to the forex trader is that you may be looking for a short trading setup in one 2 hour period and then a few hours later you are looking for a long trading setup within the very same pair. In other words, the forex trader is now looking for trading setups in the exact opposite direction. This daily price dynamic is one of the key reasons it is difficult to use any type of trend following technique to trade a currency pair.

A typical price activity within a currency pair is that a move will occur and then price will stall and flat line for 3-5 hours before another move occurs. Because of such consistent characteristics, the forex is the perfect market to use a scalp trading technique. The solid forex trader is in a trade for less than 30 minutes. A side benefit is that the trader can trade with very tight stops, which equates to minimal risk.

Once a trader starts to understand how price moves on a day to day basis within each currency pair, he quickly realizes there is rarely a reason to stay in a trade for countless hours or days and tolerate the large stops and the hours of price stagnation. It is far better to plan a trade, take the trade, take your profit, and then get out and stay on the sidelines until another setup develops.

Trend or Range?

It is a fact that as a trend trader you are going to generate a large number of losing trades before having a profitable trade. The trend trader enters the market with an objective that price will move in one direction for an extended period of time. If not, he is out of the market. The reality for a trend trader is that he will incur a number of losses before price finally moves in the direction anticipated.

Why? Trends occur roughly only 20% of the time. The remaining 80% of the time the price is range bound.

Range traders do not care about direction. Remember, the majority of time the market is range bound. Range bound traders look for smaller moves that occur frequently. Trend traders wait for larger moves that occur infrequently.

What is the reality for most individuals? They want consistent short term cash flow.

The fact is most people are more suited for sideways or range bound trading. It requires less capital, less time and offers more frequent opportunities to make a profit. The reality is most people are emotionally and financially best suited for trading the forex market on an intra-day basis and looking for small incremental moves in these consistent range bound conditions.

Although trend trading is what many traders start to focus on in the beginning, ultimately they do not have the personality, the mental stamina nor necessary trading capital to effectively and consistently trend trade.

It is important to understand the two elements to consider when pursuing a particular trading process:

1. How well do you mentally handle having a losing trade?
2. How much capital will you trade with?

Remember, trend traders have more losing trades than range bound traders. Trend trading has greater risk and so requires substantial amounts of capital to effectively trade.

The Fibonacci Trading Myth

It is very typical for trading software sellers or trading systems to claim that their particular piece of technology will allow you to find the top and bottom of every move. The belief is that markets can be traded with scientific accuracy.

The reality is that if markets moved scientifically, there would be no market.

Markets are barometers of human emotions. Millions of variables play a part.

Despite this, traders still flock to scientific theories. A popular theory now is Fibonacci numbers. This numerical sequence founded hundreds of years ago randomly identifies patterns found in nature with these numerical sequences. The reality is that there are as many natural entities that do not follow a Fibonacci sequence.

Fibonacci numbers have nothing to do with the markets. These numerical retracements and extensions, when effective, correlate to areas that are simply support and resistance.

Theories of waves, fans, pitchforks and numerical sequences are just a spin to entice individuals to believe that trading can be an absolute process, which is just not the case. Becoming a successful trader is more an art than a science.

A proven formula for success is this: Keep it simple. Price is the driving force in all markets so learn to how to interpret price free of any indicators.

A price chart is the only truly effective indicator.

The novice is enamored with trading indicators and trading theories. The experienced trader understands learning to trade is a discipline that requires very specific training. That training must teach an individual how to correctly read a price chart.

The Power of Simplicity

It has been said the genius is the ability to make the complex simple. If ever there were a catch phrase to be a guide in your trading decisions, this would be the one.

The principle known as Occam's razor is believed to be an appropriate consideration to a trader. "One should not increase beyond what is necessary, the number of entities required to achieve a solution", or the simplest solution tends to be the best one.

Stated in another form, the explanation that requires the fewest assumptions has the higher probability of being the correct one. It is astounding to observe the volumes of irrelevant information individuals digest trying to create greater accuracy in their trading decisions. In fact, this quest for more information is one key reason individuals cannot consistently make effective and accurate trading decisions.

In the last two decades that I have been personally involved in the markets, I have learned there really are only three key elements to consider when trading the forex:

- The time of day. The forex has very repetitive patterns and attributes based on the time of day you are trading.
- The price point a particular currency pair is trading at relative to the time of day.
- The size of the intra-day trading range.

Finding a trading setup requires three simple steps:

- Determine the market condition; range bound or momentum. Create a trading plan based on the condition.
- Have an entry strategy.
- Have an exit strategy.

That's it.

When trading, one wants to eliminate the unnecessary so that one may see the necessary.

However, there is a problem with this concept. Simple is no longer popular and complexity is. The perception in today's world is that complexity creates greater accuracy and efficiency. The belief is that complexity has a greater value because it costs more. If ten is good, then 20 is better and 30 is best. The current mindset is to want to buy what only is complex. When making a decision, which is easier, considering 3 elements or 30? Accuracy comes with simplicity. In trading, accuracy equates to profit.

As Mark Twain once said "The trouble with the world is not that people know too little, but that they know so many things that ain't so". A time tested rule for success in any discipline is to keep it simple.

In Search of Sasquatch, the Loch Ness Monster, Forex Robots and Other Great Myths

A former NASA engineer develops forex trading software that yields a consistent 7% return by automatically trading for you.

Does this sound too good to be true? Unfortunately it was.

If you were involved in online trading in the beginning back in 2000 you probably saw numerous infomercials promoting various trading software products. The average cost back then was $5,000. None of those companies even exist today. What is the reason for their disappearance? None of those software products worked.

The premise of these products was simple: A software would execute a trade exactly as instructed eliminating all emotions.

Think about it. In 2000 software and the internet was fast becoming an aspect of our everyday lives. We no longer needed to know how to spell, do simple arithmetic or contact a travel agent. So why shouldn't software be able to trade for us as well?

Anyone should be able to load up some trading software, connect it to their trading account and just start watching the dollars add up, right?

Centuries ago the idea of creating a machine that was capable of running on self-sustaining power was thought to be possible. You might remember it as the perpetual motion machine.

Well, to date, both are still myths.

Today the message is slightly different: Instead of software, it's called a forex robot or expert advisor. The benefit is still that these tools will automatically trade for you. The cost is much lower as well. Robots are available for less than $100 and forex brokers will give you an automated trading system for free.

Why are brokers offering these products for free? The answer is simple. These products generate a lot of trades which equal commissions in the broker's pocket. The same is true when you purchase a forex robot. The provider will tell you who you need to set up your account with because they receive a portion of the transaction cost generated by the trades the robots make. The bottom line: The incentive is that it gets the individual to trade frequently, because it is done automatically, so it is a perpetual commission machine for the broker.

Now don't get me wrong. There are some very sophisticated automated trading processes that do work. The first issue is that the individual trader is probably not going to gain access. The second issue is that these systems trade very infrequently. The benefit is that these complex trading systems monitor multiple markets and multiple entities in those markets waiting for unique anomalies to occur. In some cases, solid trading software may only have a couple of profitable trades in a 12 month period. The remaining time is spent on the sidelines out of the market. A broker could not feed his family on those commissions.

For the solo trader the recommendation is to first learn how to consistently trade manually and then once he has gained the necessary experience, use the software as a filtering tool to alert the trader of a potential opportunity. The trader can then evaluate the potential setup and make the final decision whether to place the trade.

Free or low cost automated trading products fall into the category of "In Search of the Holy Grail". No one has found it yet.

Only after you have gained the necessary trading experience, using a software as a filtering tool is a reasonable approach.

However history shows that as each new decade unfolds, we quickly forget what was marketed previously as the next great tool that will allow us to make quick money with zero effort. Time will only tell what the auto trading device of the future will be called.

The concept of turning on your computer, firing up your trading robot and then heading to the golf course while your robot is making you money defies common sense. However I am sure as you finish reading this, another ten or more such products have been sold online.

As someone once said "common sense is truly uncommon".

Key Elements Today's Forex Trader Needs To Be Versed In

The internet has changed countless areas in our day to day lives. It has not only changed the way we access information but the information we have access to as well. However in the trading world I see folks stuck in the past typically using techniques and processes developed decades ago.

The concept of using moving averages to smooth out historical price activity to discern an overall direction has been around ever since the stone tablet. The Elliott Wave Principle came out in the 30's and variations of wave theory in the 50's. The stochastic entered into the trading world in the 50's and the Relative Strength Index is now over 30 years old.

My point is that commonly used technical indicators were developed prior to the advent of the internet and more importantly before the solo trader had access to real time charting applications.

Let's face it, you would not use a device that was developed 50 years ago in probably any other area of your day to day life so why would you use it in your trading?

The answer is simple. Using what is perceived as conventional wisdom is an easy sell. Simply access this charting application, overlay this combination of indicators and now you can discern the direction of the market and fire off a trade. Brokers have been selling this myth for as long as these indicators have been in existence.

There is a huge problem with this message and the statistics show this clearly with the number of trading accounts that vaporize in losses in a short period of time.

Day to day market volatility is dramatically greater than it was 10 years ago. Think of the difference in volatility today compared to 40 or 50 years ago. It would be like trying to win the Indy 500 riding a bicycle. It just is not going to happen.

Add into the mix online trading and the instant market access from virtually anywhere on the planet, and now your bicycle has two flat tires as well.

Because of this on-the-go instantaneous access (thank you internet) people can make trading decisions instantly. That is just the solo trader. I am not even asking you to take into consideration institutional trading.

All of this growth in instant access is what creates greater and greater volatility. Trades are placed instantly, markets then react instantly, thus resulting in greater volatility. What is the primary job of all popular technical indicators? Smooth out volatility so the trader can discern direction. But what if this cannot be accomplished because price is moving too quickly? A false signal is generated. When does the trader realize it is a false signal? He realizes it only after he has lost money.

Here is a cardinal rule when using indicators: Do not attempt to use indicators in fast moving volatile markets because indicators cannot react quickly enough to assist the trader. All indicators are lagging.

The reality is today's consistently profitable solo traders are using trading processes that were not even around 5-7 years ago. Individual online trading started gaining popularity only 5-7 years ago when high speed internet access became readily accessible.

The forex market started to garner attention just about the same time. Forex has always been electronically traded so the way price moves on a day to day basis is different in the forex than in an exchange traded market. Forex is also the world's most volatile market. So when we look at a market that has always been traded electronically, has the greatest volatility and has only been actively traded by individuals for the last 5-7 years, it becomes easy to see why so many solo traders fail at trading the forex. Those failed traders are using trading processes that where developed decades ago to be applied in exchange traded low volatility markets.

Key elements today's forex trader needs to be versed in:

1. Learn to interpret day to day price action. Price action in the forex changes direction every 2-3 hours.

2. Learn to identify that the typical condition is range bound or sideways because of the constant change in the direction of price.

3. Select trading processes that are effective in sideways conditions.

4. Become competent at identifying the average size moves. Ninety percent of the moves in forex happen in less than 30-40 minutes. Price then goes flat for a couple of hours and then changes direction.

5. Have a high-probability entry strategy that uses a very tight stop.

6. Have a solid exit strategy. Know when to exit and take a profit. The concept of letting it ride does not work in the forex.

The way to get there is to become competent at interpreting real time price action. The only reliable predictive indicator available is price action. Seventy years ago when Financial World magazine first introduced Ralph Elliott's wave theory, there was no such thing as real time live charting access. Today's trader can access real time charting anywhere there is internet access.

To keep things in perspective, consider that Ralph Elliott was born in 1871. Charles Dow the father of Dow Theory was born in 1851. Dow started the whole "the trend is your friend" movement. I am sure neither of these guys would be using their techniques in today's electronic, instant access trading arena.

With electronic trading, today's trader now has the ability to learn to identify a high probability trading setup versus a low probability trading setup. These ancient indicators only allowed the trader to hopefully discern direction and be on the right side of it.

All markets will continue to become more volatile because of not only online access but the global economy we now live in, whereas decades ago we could not see what was happening in the market on a daily basis. Today we can literally watch price action minute by minute. Without real time access we were forced to stay in market positions for longer periods of time. This is why trend trading, which is now a dinosaur, was so popular. There was simply no alternative. If you wanted to trade everyone trend-traded due to limited real-time access. Today the solid online trader who has been correctly trained can achieve a profit in just a few minutes. Why stay in a trade overnight when as the globe turns any market can change direction instantly?

Remember, the reason brokers continue to promote these archaic techniques is because it is an easy sell. Indicators are simply lures that pique the gambler instinct in all of us to make us believe we can make quick and easy profits in the market simply by applying a bundle of indicators on a chart. That form of marketing has been around for decades as well. We get you in here, show bottom of the trend and we get you out here, show top of trend, and here is your huge profit. Why didn't that work when the markets melted in the sub-prime debacle or the mortgage crisis?

The harder sell is that to become a profitable trader requires time, commitment and training. Step one; you have to learn to identify solid trading setups. This takes time and exposure.

Stop listening to your broker and go out and get solid training. Would you learn to play poker with free lessons offered by a casino? Remember, the casino is just like your broker: They encourage you to start betting as soon as possible. Why do you think your broker offers all of that free training? He wants you to start betting.

Select a trading process that is centered on understanding price action with techniques that have been developed specifically for electronic trading. Stay away from one-size-fits-all programs. When you hear you can trade a process on any time frame in any market, walk away. Select a trading process that has been developed to specifically trade particular markets.

These days, you probably email people instead of writing them a letter. Why would you trade using an indicator developed 10, 20, 30 or in some cases over 50 years ago?

Forex Trader vs. Forex Investor

"Investors" put their money into stocks, real estate, and the like under the assumption that over time, the underlying investment will increase in value and that the investment will be profitable. On the other hand, "traders" take a proactive approach to when and why they put their capital into the market. Traders have a defined plan and one goal, to put their capital into the markets and take "profit."

A simple proven process to follow in achieving a goal requires 3 steps:

1. Write down what the goal is.

2. Make a detailed plan of how you are going to achieve that goal.

3. Work on it every day.

I have read an innumerable number of books on what it takes to achieve a goal. One hundred percent of those books state to "write the goal down". This simple step is missed by 19 out of 20 people. Looking at it from the other direction, only 1 out of 20 people take the time to physically write down their goals. It is no wonder so few achieve their goal.

In essence, these 19 out of 20 are just looking for things to happen in their lives. They are not planning for things to happen.

This is one of my favorite sayings: "You become what you think about most of the time". Those that continually think about the reasons why they cannot achieve their goals become those reasons. Those that continually think about ways to achieve their goals find those ways.

Consistent trading performance starts with the same 3 simple steps:

1. Write down your trading goals.

2. Create a detailed trading plan.

3. Stick to the plan.

The #1 reason individuals have inconsistent performance trading is that they do not create a solid written trading plan to work from.

Most traders typically look at a particular currency pair or pairs, blind to the conditions, and make a quick emotional justification of why they are going to place a trade and do it. They are literally trading from the seat of their pants. What are the results of this practice over time? You make money, you then give it back, and as time progresses you give back more than you make.

The first rule to follow: Plan your trade, trade your plan.

Here are the 6 P's of trading: Proper prior planning prevents poor performance.

We wait for the market to come to us. We plan trades. We do not just look for trades. To be able to do this, one must learn via the correct training how to interpret price action and understand market conditions.

In short, the trader evaluates a particular currency pair and then sets an alarm to be notified when price is in the correct area for a high probability trade. The trader has zero risk at this point. He is waiting for a high probability setup to develop.

When the alarm goes off, the trader evaluates the new condition and follows a simple step-by-step process to ensure he gets the correct confirmation that he is trading a high probability setup. He then places the trade.

Working first from the vantage point of planning and waiting, the trader can then use a very tight stop to place a trade.

This process from beginning to end is a proven formula for trading success by trading only high probability setups.

The trader with the plan may have to wait a couple of hours for the alarm to go off. When it does, he trades with certainty and confidence. With wireless technology, that planned trade can be executed from a smartphone, netbook or laptop.

Imagine this scenario: After creating your trading plan, you set an alarm to be notified by text message or email when your setup is beginning to develop. The alarm goes off and you place the trade directly on your smartphone. You make it a 3 lot trade with a net 10 pip profit target for a total trade gain of 30 pips.

Ten minutes later your profit is achieved and you just made $300.

The professional trader is out of the market more than he is in. He only wants to trade only high probability setups; he is focused on quality over quantity. Ultimately he reaches a level of experience such that he just needs one solid setup a day and trades multiple lots on that setup. He works less, and he also has less stress and anxiety when trading **because he trades with certainty.**

The novice trader is always in the market nursing poor trades along by moving his stop farther out and hoping he gets "lucky" bouncing from one process to the next. He never achieves a level of mastery at any one process.

He is not trading. He is gambling.

The novice trader is hoping things will end in his favor. He trades with lots of stress and anxiety and is never sure if the trade will be profitable. He trades with only hope and luck, just as a gambler does in a casino.

The novice feels he should always be trading; the professional waits for the market to come to him.

The first step towards successful trading is to get solid training in how to create a trading plan.

Low Risk Forex Trading

As a trader, getting stopped out is just part of the cost of doing business. I find that this is a seldom addressed area in today's internet driven "get rich overnight trading the forex" arena. But in fact, it should be the first thing one considers when evaluating a trading program.

I am a firm believer in the "KISS" principle: Keep it simple s*&%id.

Stop Placement 101:

You need to use very large stops (greater risk) when trading a trend following technique. The larger the profit target, so too is the larger the stop that needs to be used. When trading a scalping technique you can use a very small stop (less risk). The smaller the profit target, the tighter the stop.

Why? If you are attempting to go for a larger profit target, you are going to be in a trade for a longer period of time. In order to overcome the standard pullbacks and price fluctuations that occur when one stays in a trade for an extended period of time, you need a larger stop. This style of trading is very common place in markets where the directional bias is very consistent.

One of the key characteristics of the forex market that is different than other markets is that the directional bias is constantly shifting. In one 3 hour period you may be looking for a long trade and in the next 3 hour period you may be looking for a short trade on the very same currency pair. What this means to the trader who is attempting to trade a trend following technique in the forex is that he will need to use very large stops, typically a minimum of 100 pips or more in most cases.

Once again, the reason for this is because of the constant shift in the directional bias. This is why many perceive the forex to be a "risky" market to trade.

The forex is a great market to trade, but it is not just a good market to trade a trend following technique. Trend following technique is not the technique for you if you cannot handle the large stops and the countless hours you are stuck in a trade waiting for the bias to shift back in your favor.

The forex market is the perfect market to trade on an intra-day basis. You can use a tight stop and you do not have to hold on to a trade for countless hours. A side benefit of trading these smaller intra-day moves is that it is less emotionally taxing.

One of the benefits of learning to trade a scalping methodology is that you use a 10 pip stop including the transaction cost. That is low risk trading.

In any other business endeavor, if I asked you whether would you prefer to earn $500 in 30 minutes or in 12-14 hours, the answer would be obvious. But for some reason traders feel that there is a benefit to holding on to a trade for extended periods of time. Trend followers risk more and work harder to earn money trading the forex. Scalpers can earn the same or more than trend followers with less risk and only committing a fraction of the time.

Here is another way to look at it. Let's look at a currency pair that has a daily trading range of 75 pips. Which is easier? Learning to consistently find 10-20 pips of profit in a consistent 75 pip range or to find the entire 75 pips? Which is less work? Once again, the answer is obvious.

Remember, one 5 lot net 10 pip trade equals 50 pips or $500 in profit and typically can be realized in 30 minutes or less.

Forex Trading Using Technical Analysis

Technical analysis is the interpretation of price action through the use of charts and indicators.

Indicators have a very specific place in trading. The majority of popular indicators do not perform consistently in volatile conditions. There is too much whipsaw or up and down price activity. Because of this, indicators are best used on larger time frames and trading in markets with low volatility.

For this reason many individuals steer away from volatile markets. The reality is volatility is a good thing when traded correctly. Volatility equates to more profit taking opportunities, and the forex is the world's most volatile market. A key feature of the forex market is consistent price swings in very short periods of time. For the trader, this equates to frequent short term profit taking opportunities. As one who trades technically based on price, you embrace this volatility. As a technical trader you do not care what the reason is behind this volatility. You just want to be able to understand the movement and, more importantly, take advantage of it.

It is important to understand that this same volatility can get a trader into trouble if he trades using an incorrect time frame, so using the correct time frame is critical to trading successfully.

Technical analysis operates on the theory that price reflects all known factors affecting supply and demand at that time. Hence a price chart is all we need to use to identify good trading setups.

Markets are a reflection of human emotion. People make and move markets, not balance sheets. So by developing the skill to interpret price action, you develop an understanding of the view of all those trading it.

A price charts tells us what has happened in the past. And since the past tends to repeat itself, it can give us an indication of what might happen in the future.

In fact, technical analysis is the most powerful trading tool an individual can use. And because of this, technical analysis provides the framework for a systematic approach to trading. More importantly, it gives us the confidence to make our trading decisions.

Technical analysis provides precise mechanisms for trade entry and exit. Strategies that are based on technical analysis afford the trader higher probability trading opportunities.

There are countless patterns and strategies that fall under the umbrella of technical analysis. It is important to be trained in how to select the correct strategy to apply to the current market condition you are monitoring as well as how to select the correct time frame to trading in.

Trade the Forex with the Correct Time Frame

Prior to electronic trading, before there was free real-time online access to charting, selecting a time frame to trade with was a non-issue. Standard operating procedure was to simply look at a daily chart and end of day activity. Today this is no longer the case. With easy access to real-time charting, selecting the correct time frame is an important element to a trader's success.

Old school market theory was to always use a large time frame. This mindset was common because the stand alone trader could not access real time charting. In fact, when electronic trading started to gain attention in the late 90's, it was common for traders to spend in excess of $500 a month just to subscribe to a stand-alone charting application. There were no alternatives like there are today.

In those days a common scenario was to simply take standard investing practices and scale those concepts down to trading. We now know the concepts that make a solid trader are not the same concepts that we would apply to investing.

Another common misconception was that you could trade any process in any market on any time frame. The biggest flaw with this idea is that not all markets or trading entities move in the same fashion. Attempting to apply a trading process developed for highly volatile entity like the forex to a low volatile entity or vice versa is just not going to work. Unfortunately we still see today this "one size fits all" trading mentality heavily marketed on the internet. This one misconception is the single biggest contributor to the high failure rate of most traders.

The "one size fits all" trading concept is an easy sell: Buy XYZ trading program and trade it long term or short term on virtually any market. But once the trader gets a modicum of experience he quickly realizes that this thought process literally defies common sense.

The trader in the know understands that we now have the ability to not only select a process that has been developed to trade specific markets, but an integral part of what makes a trading process successful is making sure it is used on the correct time frame.

The key to selecting a time frame is to start small. After all, today's online trader has the luxury of looking at price action in small increments as opposed to pre-online trading days. Keep in mind that the single biggest difference between a trader's mindset and investor's mindset is that the trader understands his goal is to spend the absolute least amount of time possible in the market while yielding the absolute most amount of profit.

The investor needs time on his side to overcome the day-to-day market fluctuations and hopes that over time he ends up with more money than he started. Remember, the trader is taking advantage of those daily market fluctuations. The trader asks, why stay in a position overnight and be exposed to those fluctuations without the ability to manage the process? It is simply too much risk.

With today's global economy and easy online access to the markets, folks are quickly realizing that it is just way too risky to be in the markets overnight or for extended periods of time. The numbers are growing exponentially of those who favor the mindset of get in, get a profit and get out; a short term trading mentality. This is a good thing for traders. This new market sentiment is creating ever more short term trading opportunities.

If you want to maximize your potential for profit in the shortest period of time, you need to select a market that has huge volume and lots of volatility.

Significant volume is required so that there is less likelihood that any one entity controls the market and so that your trade has greater probability of being executed as intended.

Volatility is required so that you actually have something to trade. Think of volatility as extreme price fluctuations that occur frequently. That condition makes investors lose sleep, but it's the absolute best condition for a trader.

In order to be a solid trader you have to think like a trader, not an investor.

Hands down, the world's largest and most volatile market is the forex, the absolute perfect market to trade online.

If you select a time frame that is too small, say for instance a 1 minute chart, there is just too much back and forth activity to discern a solid trading setup. This is a form of what traders call whipsaw. So you need to select a time frame that smoothes out some of this whipsaw or back and forth movement. However we do not want to pick a time frame that is too large because then we will miss trading opportunities. The sweet spot to be able to realize maximum potential profits in the shortest period of time is the 10 minute chart.

In the forex we can often take advantage of a 100 pip move in one 10 minute increment. Then a common occurrence is that price goes flat for 30-60 minutes and then changes direction, which means another potential trading opportunity.

Another key benefit of trading on a 10 minute chart is it allows the trader to use a very small or tight stop to minimize risk. In fact, another difference between a trader and an investor is that a trader uses stops to protect his capital and minimize his risk. An investor just hopes price will come back in his favor over time should price go against them.

A key element to realize at this point is that if we were to use a larger time frame our stop would also have to be increased. In forex the price action changes so quickly that increasing the stop size exposes the solo trader to too much risk.

The bottom line is using a 10 minute time increment creates a winning formula of maximum profit in the shortest time period while also reducing risk to its tightest possible tolerance.

If you're thinking like a trader you quickly realize that even a 10 or 20 pip move with a very tight stop is the smartest and safest way to go. If you want to increase your profits you simply trade multiple lots.

It is critical to never violate this cardinal rule of trading: Realize your profit objective in the shortest possible time with the least amount of risk. Another way to look at it is, get in, get positive and get out.

Because the forex is the world's most volatile market, price is constantly changing direction unlike slower, less volatile markets. That is why the trader must select a trading process that work consistently in that type of condition. The first element in that process is selecting the correct time frame.

Three Things That Will Make You a Solid Forex Trader

If I could name only three things necessary to become a successful trader, these would be it:

1. Focus on quality of trading, not quantity of trading.

The top statistical reason why forex traders cannot hold onto any profits they make is over-trading. Let's face it, forex brokers make money based on how much trading you do. The more you trade, the more money they make. So what is their objective? It is to get you to trade as frequently as possible. How do they do this? They pummel you with as much free information as they can. The majority of this information is useless for trading any currency pair on a day to day basis.

So how can you, the forex trader, keep those profits? Cut back on the quantity of trading you do. Once again, it is statistically shown that the trader who minimizes the number of trades he places will hold onto his profits for a longer period of time than the one who trades too frequently.

So how do you accomplish this? You do so by learning that just because you are in front of your computer does not mean there is always a solid trading opportunity in front of you. The solid, consistent trader always trades with the mindset of "always look for a reason not to place a trade".

Keep in mind, all a forex broker is a salesman. That's it, pure and simple.

2. Realize you're a forex trader, not a forex gambler.

The gambler goes into a casino with a fistful of dollars ready to bet, relying solely on hope and luck. He has no plan. He has no process. He has no system. He is not a professional gamer who works with a tried and true system. He is a gambler, at best armed with some bits and pieces of free information that he has gleaned from the internet, e-books and friendly advice.

This is the same description of 80% of the forex traders out there. They turn on their computer and log into their trading platform with the sole mission of firing off a trade as soon as possible. The two key factors they are relying on are the same; hope and luck.

Let's say you want to become a professional gamer. Let's pick poker. What makes sense, to get free lessons from a casino? Remember, the casino's mission is to get you to the table and betting as soon as possible. That is why the casinos offer free lessons. The casinos know that the sooner they entice you play, the sooner they start making money off of you.

Instead of free casino lessons, how about seeking out paid-for training from a professional poker player? Certainly there is a financial commitment and a time commitment. But this route yields a much higher probability that you will move onto become a successful poker player.

All a forex brokerage firm is a casino. With the same incentives as a casino, a brokerage firm offers free training to get you to trade as soon as possible so they can make money from the transaction cost.

Do you want to be a solid, consistent trader? Seek out professional training. You know the old saying, "you get what you pay for". So do not expect to make thousands and thousands of dollars from a $500 training program. Look for a solid, professional forex training program with positive ratings when you do an online search.

3. First focus on preserving your capital. Then focus on growing your capital.

The concept sounds simple and obvious. However, most forex traders never think from the paradigm of preserving capital first. All they want to do is trade. To become a successful trader, apply the cardinal rule of the consistently profitable forex trader: Plan your trade and trade your plan. The forex trader who ends the week, the month and the year in the positive knows exactly what he will consider trading and what he will pass on. He is just like the professional poker player. The professional poker player does not bet on every hand. He waits for a high probability hand to come his way before he is willing to put his money on the table. He works from the premise of "preserve and grow your capital". The professional forex trader does the exact same thing; he waits for a high probability trading setup to develop. No solid winning setup, no trade.

How does he learn to identify a winning trading setup? He learns by paying for professional training.

The gambler is always looking for the get rich quick scheme, the Holy Grail, the magic formula, which we all know does not exist. He is looking for immediate gratification, the instant success.

In seeking out professional training to trade the forex, keep this in mind: If the hype around a product or program defies common sense, then it is simply too good to be true.

There is no secret on how to become a successful forex trader. Successful forex traders understand that learning how to trade is no different than learning any other discipline. Follow the tried and true path of getting solid training.

Learn to Trade the Forex: The 3 Steps to a Profitable Trade

Trading is very simple in concept: just buy and sell. But to properly trade the forex or any market, one of the first aspects a trader realizes is that each step of a trade is a small but concise process in itself that requires attention.

The proper implementation of each of these steps is what determines whether the trade is actually profitable, and the training program at The Forex Trading Institute precisely teaches you how to follow these steps.

Step One: Determine Market Direction

Markets can trend, go up or down, or they can be sideways. In the forex, the market is in sideways conditions 90% of the time, so the first step for a forex trader should be to assume that an individual currency pair is in a sideways range. After making this assumption, a range bound strategy would be ideal to apply to that currency pair.

The advantage is that range bound strategies work on both sideways and trending markets. Trending strategies only work when there is a trend in the market, which is only 10% of the time. Thinslice Trading teaches you four strategies designed to make profit in sideways markets, keeping in mind that they work in trending markets as well.

Step Two: Entry strategy

A precise entry strategy ensures that the trader is able to identify a clear entry point based on a set of rules. This entry strategy should be a black and white process; either the setup is a good trade, or it is not.

Clearly following the appropriate rules to identify a good trading setup is what will result in a higher probability of the trade actually working out. The Forex Trading Institute's training program is a simple but effective approach. It clearly identifies if the setup is a good entry point or not, making it easy for the student to clearly understand how to identify good trading opportunities.

Step Three: Exit strategy

This is how the trader gets paid. This step is just as important as the entry strategy. A fixed profit objective of 10 to 30 pips is a reasonable profit objective when the average price move of a currency pair is 30-50 pips. That is the goal of the forex trading strategies used in Thinslice Trading. This is what is known as a scalping method.

By using a scalping methodology, or trying to get a piece of a price move instead of the complete move, Thinslice Trading is able to increase the chances of the trade succeeding. Remember that 90% of the time, a currency pair is in a range bound condition. The only way to consistently make a profit in this condition is by trading a scalping technique.

Most beginning traders try to take a trade to the top or bottom of a move, which usually leads to a losing trade. The solid forex trader wants to scalp a high probability section of the move.

Following these three steps in the way The Forex Trading Institute instructs its traders, by properly identifying the trading condition of a particular currency pair and having a clear entry and exit strategy, is the mark of a solid forex trader.

Many traders tend to overlook the details of each step, or sometimes overcomplicate each step, which leads to losing trades.

The Range and Reversal Trade

Since the predominant trading condition of the six major currency pairs is range bound, the range and reversal trade is a solid trading setup to learn as one of your core trading setups.

The six major pairs are EUR/USD, GBP/USD, USD/JPY, USD/CHF, AUD/USD and USD/CAD. These are consistently the most frequently traded currency pairs.

We can identify a trading range or sideways conditions by viewing a daily chart. You can look at diagram 1.1 below to see what a trading range looks like.

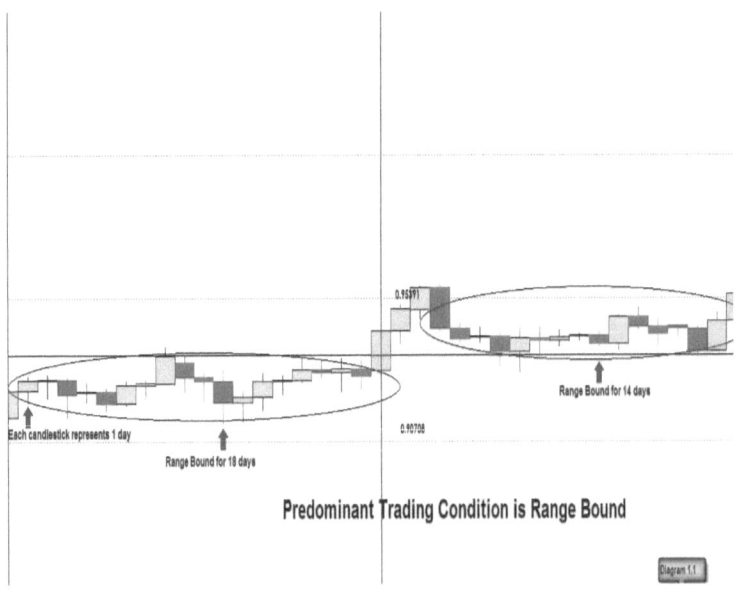

A few key points to keep in mind:

1. We need a minimum of two days to begin to discern range bound conditions. A simple way to learn to identify a range is to look at a daily chart and notate today's high and low on the daily chart. Then wait 24 hours and compare the previous day's high and low to the current day's high and low. Moving forward you can begin to discern a top and or bottom of range by comparing current daily high and low to the last few days' high and low. Note that some of the currency pairs have more discernible ranges than others. That's why you should get in the habit of looking at all six pairs mentioned above. Typically after a few days, it is easy to identify sideways price action on the daily chart.
2. On occasion you will see on a pair where the top of range is much easier to identify than the bottom or vice versa. You want to select the pair that has a clear identifiable top or bottom of range. Ideally select a pair in which both the top and the bottom of range are easy to see.
3. Remember that range bound conditions are very predominant so it makes sense to wait as many days as necessary for a solid, easy to identify range to develop. Two to 3 days is the minimum criteria.

Once you have identified a solid range on the daily chart, you are now ready to create your trading plan on the 10 minute chart.

All charting applications have some type of a drawing tool. Draw a horizontal line on your daily chart at the top of range and another line at the bottom of range. Once you have drawn these lines, change your time frame to 10 minutes so that you can view your horizontal lines in the 10 minute chart. The lines should transfer over from the daily chart.

Let's now plan for a reversal trade at the top of range on the 10 minute chart.

Note that this reversal activity typically occurs within the last hour of the trading session you are trading in.

Working on the 10 minute chart, wait for price to move to your horizontal line that indicates the top of range. We need the price to stop in the vicinity of that horizontal line and then develop an identifiable support level. Once that level of support is established, you can set your entry to trigger when price clears the support. See diagram 1.2 below for an illustration.

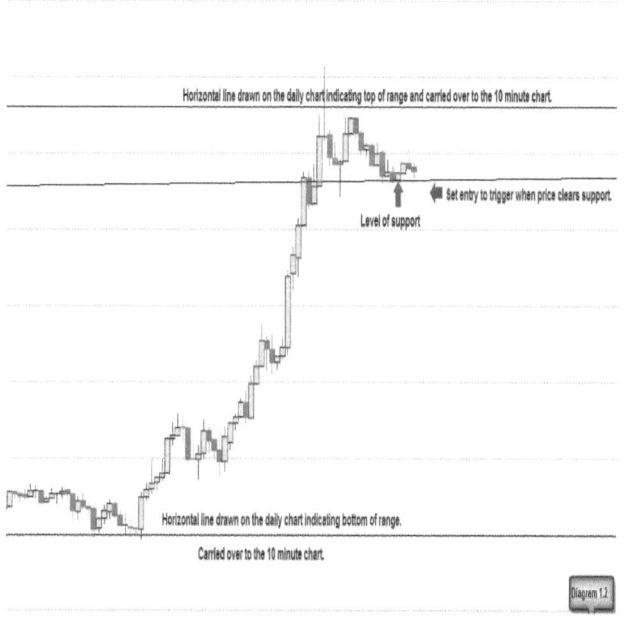

Remember, having a precise entry strategy ensures that the trader is able to identify a clear entry point based on a set of rules. This entry strategy should be a black and white process.

The more precise the entry strategy is, the higher the probability that the trade will move in the correct direction.

At Thinslice Trading, we teach you a precise entry strategy down to the correct entry minute.

The above example given was trading a reversal from the top of range. To trade the reversal at the bottom of range, follow the same process but look for identifiable resistance in place of the support since you are now trading in the other direction. See diagram 1.3 for an illustration of this second example.

Diagram 1.3

The last step is having a pre-determined exit point. The average size move for the major currency pairs is about 30 pips. A simple rule of thumb is to establish a predetermined profit target of one-half of the average size of a move. This would equal 15 pips, and less transaction cost puts your profit target at 10-12 pips.

A proven formula for success is to make small consistent gains repeatedly. The conservative trader who follows this guideline makes on average 10 times more profit over the same period of time as the trader who is always looking to capitalize on a "home run" move.

Remember, one net 10 pip trade with 5 lots equal $500. Do that 4 times a week and that multiplies this simple action to $2,000. Repeat over 50 weeks and that equates to six figures.

Warning: Not Everyone Is Capable of Becoming a Solid Forex Trader

Not everyone is capable of becoming a consistent trader. Learning to become a trader is no different than learning any other discipline. It takes time, training, commitment and discipline.

It is a myth that there is some trading product available that allows for quick and easy profits. Eight out of 10 people fail because they believe this myth.

It does not matter whether you choose to trade using a technology based program or by learning to understand price action. It does not matter whether you prefer long-term or short-term trading. In all cases, you need to take the time to learn how each market works. There is no such thing as a universal product that can make money in any market or on any time frame.

If all it took was a few hundred bucks and a set of DVD's or a magical indicator package to make money, everyone would be trading successfully.

If you are looking for that "magic" trading product, you are better off going to a casino or playing the lottery. If you are looking to make instant "big bucks", spend your time and money on low-cost trading gimmicks. You have a higher chance of success playing roulette in a casino.

Most folks have a huge misconception as to what the daily function of a stand-alone trader is. Let me break it down for you. Your job is to create a trading plan that requires a high probability trading setup to develop based on your trading rules and criteria and then execute that trade based on your trading plan. If the plan does not develop correctly, there is no trade.

You are not a macro-economist or an analyst.

Just because you turn on your computer and trade does not mean at that point in time there is something worth trading.

Your objective is to preserve your capital and consider only trading high probability setups in the best conditions.

There are a number of programs and products out there that lead you to believe anyone can trade successfully and that you can trade anytime you feel like turning on your computer. This is a fallacy.

Once again, if it was that easy everyone would be making money trading and the statistic would be 80% are successful and 20% fail. Unfortunately that is not the case.

First you need to select a trading process that matches your personality and, more importantly, the amount of trading capital you have available.

If you are trading with less than $10,000 you need to select a process that trains you to trade small intra-day moves with tight stops and small profit targets. You simply cannot afford to trade with large stops and look for big moves. Here is a simple rule of thumb to follow when selecting a trading process: Lower risk trades occur on smaller time frames and happen more frequently. Higher risk trades develop over larger time frames and occur less frequently. If you only have $10,000 or less, in order to survive and stay around for a while, you need to trade with minimal risk. You do not have the money to look for high risk trades.

Another point to consider is this: I never met a broker who did not want to make a lot of money. All brokers are commissioned licensed salesmen. Their objectives are very straight forward: Get you to open an account as soon as possible and then trade as much as possible. Their commissions are based on how much you trade, period. Whether you win or lose, they make money only if you trade. Naturally, to achieve their objective, they are going to offer you all the free incentives they can to stimulate you to trade as much as possible. Remember that their success is measured by how much you trade, not by how successful your trading is. The reason brokers are licensed and regulated is because history has shown they will tell you anything so they can make money. Plain and simple.

So if your plan was to let your broker teach you to trade via his free training programs, I encourage you to reconsider that plan.

Trading can be a lucrative profession. Just as most independent businesses fail, so too most traders. It all boils down to one reason. The failures were due to looking for immediate gratification and instant success.

In order to be in the winning 20%, you need to make sure you do not do what the losing 80% are doing.

Remember, successful traders do what unsuccessful traders refuse to do. Solid disciplined traders are not looking for shortcuts. They are willing to make the commitment and sacrifices necessary to achieve their goals. They understand the difference between a gambler's mindset and a trader's mindset. Here is a winning trading formula: Make small consistent gains and build those gains over time. Here is a losing trading formula: Jump into the market looking for the big move and then rely solely on hope and luck to achieve your profit.

Someone once said "common sense is an uncommon thing." This statement epitomizes the failed trader; they simply lack common sense. Remember, not everyone has what it takes to become a successful trader.

www.ingramcontent.com/pod-product-compliance
Lightning Source LLC
Chambersburg PA
CBHW022132170526
45157CB00004B/1853